This book belongs to:

. . . .

. . . .

Table of content:

Slanted Angle Lined Guide

Alphabet Practice Sheets

Dot Grid Paper Sheets

112

Thank you!

We really appreciate your purchase.
We hope you're happy with everything

**To help us make better books,
We'd love it if you could take a minute
to leave a 5-star review on amazon.**

_____

How to leave us a review?

1- Go to **Amazon.com/ryp** or scan this QR code
2- Scroll to this book.
3- Select star rating & write a review.

Thanks in advance for your help!

Made in the USA
Monee, IL
27 July 2024

62726244R00070